8 PRACTICAL STEPS TO SELF-FEED PRODUCTION FOR YOUR CHICKEN:
(operation do it yourself)

Emmanuel Jacob

Table of contents

Step 1

OBTAIN A BALANCED FEED FORMULA

GROWER MASH FORMULA

Maize 48kg

Wheat bran 32kg

Soybean meal (SBM) 12.60kg

Lysine 0.25kg (250g)

Methionine 0.30kg (300g)

Salt 0.50kg (500g)

Vitamin Premix 0.25kg (250g)

Bone meal 3kg

Limestone 3kg

Enzymes 0.025kg (25g)

Toxic binder 0.10kg (100g)

Crude Protein (cp): 16.5%

Metabolizable energy (ME) 2793.46 Kcal/kg

Oh yes, that's the beginning of producing balanced feed for your chicken.

A feed formula is a stated animal ration's fact expressed in values of individual ingredients required to meet the animal's desired nutritional requirements.

A simple arithmetic process known as feed formulation is used to generate an animal feed formula.

A balanced feed formula must answer the following questions:

Is the feed formula suitable for the age of the chicken? - age is often used to categorize the type of feed to be fed to chicken. We have two broiler age categories: broiler starter (0-4 weeks) and broiler finisher (5-disposal), and three pullet age categories: chick mash (0-8 weeks), grower mash (9-19 weeks), and layers mash (Point of lay to disposal)

Are the ingredients listed in the formula easily accessible and available in your locality? - always consider the availability of ingredients. Are they always available? Consistent availability of ingredients will keep you from changing your formula. Changing formula from time to time will have a negative impact on your chicken, especially laying birds.

What's the purpose of raising the chicken? Is it for eggs, meat production, or breeding...?

What are the basic nutritional requirements of the chicken in terms of crude protein, energy, fiber, calcium, and phosphorus?...

What are the present weather conditions? The weather has a significant impact on feed production, particularly in determining the energy level of the feed. Because for example, broilers require more metabolizable energy (ME) to meet up in the body's system in the cold season, you will likely increase the energy content of feed in the cold season and decrease it in the extremely hot season for chicken.

Does the formula sum up to 100%/kg? A balanced feed formula usually sums up to 100kg or its equivalent, it's then multiplied out to other desired quantities.

500kg = multiply each ingredient by 5

1000kg (1 ton) = multiply each ingredient by 10

2000kg (2 tons) = multiply each ingredient by 20...

Here are samples of balanced feed formula (extract from my book PREPARED ANIMALS' FEED FORMULA)

THE BROILER STARTER FORMULA

Maize 55kg

Wheat bran 3kg

Soybean meal (SBM) 18kg

Soy full fat 18.48kg

Fish meal 3kg (72% cp)

Lysine 0.25kg (250g)

Methionine 0.30kg (300g)

Salt 0.50kg (500g)

Vitamin Premix 0.25kg (250g)

Bone meal 0.50kg (500g)

Limestone 0.50kg (500g)

Enzymes 0.025kg (25g)

Toxic binder 0.10kg (100g)

Neobron 0.10kg (100g)

Crude Protein (cp): 23.35%

Metabolizable energy (ME) 3301 Kcal/kg

THE CHICK MASH FORMULA (0-8 WEEKS)

Maize 55kg

Wheat bran 3kg

Soybean meal (SBM) 23.23kg

Soybean cake (SBC) 14.25kg

Lysine 0.25kg (250g)

Methionine 0.30kg (300g)

Salt 0.50kg (500g)

Vitamin Premix 0.25kg (250g)

Bone meal 1.50kg (1500g)

Limestone 1.50kg (1500g)

Enzymes 0.025kg (25g)

Neobron 0.10kg (100g)

Toxic binder 0.10kg (100g)

Crude Protein (cp): 22.53%

Metabolizable energy (ME) 3263.36 Kcal/kg

Balanced feed formula is available in the book below. Order it here along with this book.

ALL ANIMALS' FEED FORMULA

ACCESS TO BALANCED FEED FORMULA IS THE PANACEA TO PRODUCTIVE ANIMAL PRODUCTION ENTERPRISE

Emmanuel Jacob

<u>**We shall use the first formula (broiler starter mash) as a case study in the 7 steps of self-feed production for your chicken.**</u>

Step 2

CARRY OUT PROXIMATE ANALYSIS OF YOUR INGREDIENTS

Proximate analysis is a laboratory quantitative test that employs a variety of scientific techniques to determine the percentage of nutrients present in various ingredients.

Failure to carry out proximate analysis of ingredients that made up your formula is one of the major reasons for the production of poor feed. Feed formulation is calculated based on the proximate analysis of ingredients used at arriving at the nutritional requirements of the animal in question.

you are bound to produce less quality feed without good proximate analysis. The safe and best way to ascertain the

nutritional content of feed ingredients is through proximate analysis. The best practice in feed production is to carry out the proximate analysis of ingredients involved in the feed formula.

I understand the fact that carrying out proximate analysis may be a serious challenge for many local farmers due to the lack of access to laboratories and the cost of carrying out proximate analysis for each ingredient can be unbearable; nevertheless, this is the best practice in producing balanced feed.

Failure to determine the proximate analysis of ingredients forces many of us to rely on expert estimates (which is also acceptable). However, when relying on expert estimates, you will be on the safe side if you assume to work with the lowest values generated for each ingredient. For example, you may have seen maize proximate analysis ranging from 7-10% cp. When calculating your feed formula, it is preferable and safer to use a cp of 7%. The same logic should apply to other ingredients.

Step 3

SOURCE FOR RAW MATERIALS

Raw materials are otherwise known as feed ingredients.

Sourcing for raw materials is very critical to balanced feed production. The following should come to mind when sourcing raw materials:

✓ Are the ingredients readily available and affordable? Ingredients for feed production should be available year-round to prevent unnecessary changes in feed formula.

✓ Can you identify the ingredients? - know your ingredients! Can you identify maize, soybean, groundnut cake, palm kernel cake, or fish meal?... You must be able to identify feed ingredients:

✓ By seeing

✓ By smells

✓ By touch

✓ By color

✓ Are the ingredients in the right moisture content level? Don't buy damp ingredients. All ingredients must be below 10% moisture content. Order for moisture tester to check the moisture content of feed ingredients.

Moisture tester

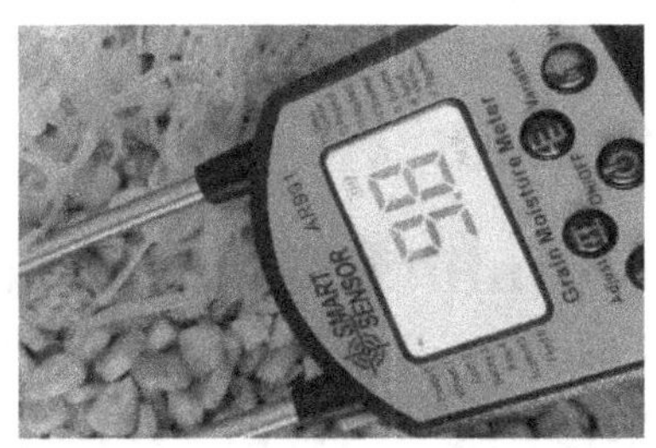

The good moisture content of 9.8%

✓ Are the ingredients free from weevils infestation? You must avoid weevils-infested maize.

✓ Are the ingredients rancid? Most oil-based ingredients will easily go rancid if unused for a long time.

Rancidification is the process of complete or incomplete autoxidation or hydrolysis of fats and oils when exposed to air, light, moisture, or bacterial action, producing short-chain aldehydes, ketones, and free fatty acids. When these processes occur in food, undesirable odors and flavors can result.

Don't order milled ingredients. You are on the safer side of unadulterated feed ingredients if you avoid buying already milled ingredients. Go for whole ingredients and mill it by yourself. In some cases, milled ingredients are adulterated.

Source for your ingredients during the harvesting season. Raw materials are usually cheaper to buy during the harvesting season. To produce cheaper feed, you must make use of this opportunity to stock a good quantity of your raw materials during harvesting season. However, you must make sure you dry them to an expected moisture content of 10% before using them.

Don't use newly harvested maize for feed production. Newly harvested maize can expose your chicken to chronic respiratory disease (CRD)

PICTORIAL SAMPLES OF FEED INGREDIENTS

Below are samples of some feed ingredients.

White maize.

Yellow maize

Groundnut cake

Soybean meal

**Maize bran
wheat bran**

•

Blood meal

Soybean cake

Bone: make use of the whitish ones

Step 4

CLEANING OF INGREDIENTS
Cleaning your ingredients is the art of picking off foreign objects from your ingredients. This is very essential in order to avoid all objects that could constitute health hazards to your chicken and also affect the overall nutritional value of your feed.

REASONS FOR CLEANING RAW MATERIALS

Grain preservatives can be detected. In the above picture camphor used as a preservative was discovered. This could have to constitute health hazards to your chicken.

Phostoxin discovered - phostoxin is one of the preservatives used to preserve maize against weevils' infestation

**Foreign objects are removed from
your ingredients during cleaning.**

Step 5

PROCESSING OF INGREDIENTS
Processing of ingredients enhances their nutritional values.
Ingredients processing means altering the physical (and sometimes chemical) nature of feed ingredients to optimize their utilization by animals.
You can locally process your feed ingredients via the application of heat in most cases.
Benefits of ingredients processing include
It improves feed digestibility
Enhances the nutritional value of the ingredients
Make it easier to mix with other ingredients

Processing destroys anti-nutritional elements present in certain feed ingredients
Processing is one of the means of preserving the feed ingredients against mold, and insects... (preserves ingredients longevity)
Certain ingredients that require processing before inclusion in feed production are:
SOYA FULL FAT

This is done locally by pouring the soya full fat into a frying pan and toasting it until it turns brownish and the back coat becomes easy to peel off. Full fat contains an anti-nutritional element called trypsin present at the back coat of the seed; this is destroyed through the application of heat and it becomes safe for chicken consumption.
This can be done mechanically by the use of a toaster machine.

RAW BLOOD
Raw blood is processed into a blood meal by boiling the blood until coagulation takes place. The coagulated blood is then dried and ground to power to become blood meal

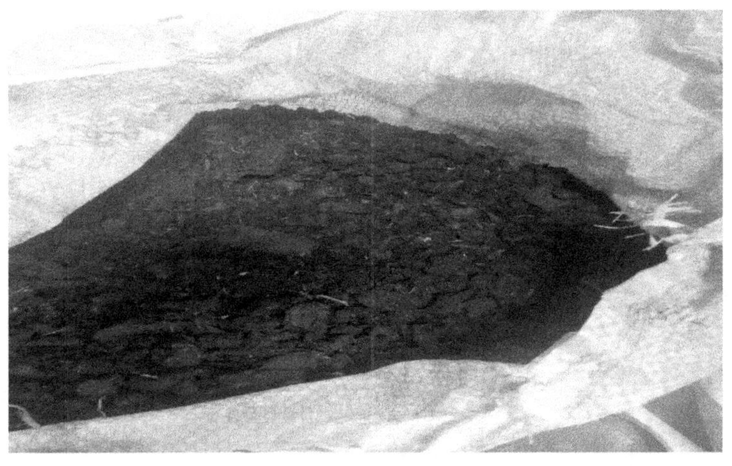

SOYBEAN MEAL

It's been processed industrially in most cases. Extracting the oil from the flakes is by the solvent extraction process. The bye product called the meals is then sold as a soya bean meal for feed production. The same thing goes for groundnut cake.

BONE

Collected bones from the abattoir are burnt until it becomes a whitish bristle. This is then crushed to become a bone meal.
Make use of the whitish bones. Avoid the burnt blackish ones.

Step 6

WEIGHING OF INGREDIENTS

At the weighing stage, you are practically interpreting your formula on paper to the physical feed for your chicken. It then means that you have to be very careful in handling your weighing scale else you might be producing feed different from what you have on paper through wrong weighing or faulty scale.

We have two types of weighing scales: the analog and the digital scale.

Digital scale is preferred because of its higher accuracy.

We also have lesser capacity-sensitive digital scales. Some are just 5kg in capacity. They are good for measuring light ingredients like additives (lysine, methionine, salt, vitamin premix...)

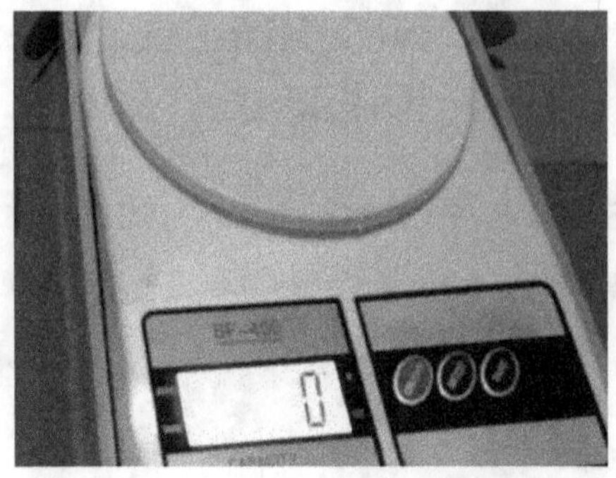

You must be very careful at the point of weighing your ingredients because the real act of feed production starts from here.
You should be able to convert weight in grams to kilograms and vice versa where necessary.
Weighing is one of the most tedious aspects of feed production.
Weighing should be done systematically; from your formula tick each ingredient as you weigh, else you might omit an ingredient or weigh some ingredients twice. Make

sure you weigh all ingredients before crushing them.
Let us look at this formula

THE BROILER STARTER FORMULA

Maize 55kg

Wheat bran 3kg

Soybean meal (SBM) 18kg

Soy full fat 18.48kg (18kg.480g)

Fish meal 3kg (72% cp)

Lysine 0.25kg (250g)

Methionine 0.30kg (300g)

Salt 0.50kg (500g)

Vitamin Premix 0.25kg (250g)

Bone meal 0.50kg (500g)

Limestone 0.50kg (500g)

Enzymes 0.025kg (25g)

Toxic binder 0.10kg (100g)

Neobron 0.10kg (100g)

Crude Protein (cp): 23.35%

Metabolizable energy (ME) 3301 Kcal/kg

The formula is for 100kg feed

If I want to produce the feed in 500kg (half a ton), each ingredient will be multiplied by 5

1 ton, each ingredient will be multiplied by 10

2 tons, each ingredient will be multiplied by 20

Step 7

CRUSHING OF INGREDIENTS

This is another critical aspect of feed production.

This is an act of running your ingredients through a pulverizer or crusher to break them down to the desired particle sizes.

Crushing of ingredients must be done using the same sieve for all the ingredients for uniformity.

All ingredients must pass through the crusher, except the additives (lysine, methionine, salt, vitamin premix...)

Your crusher should be with a changeable sieve. This implies that you should be able to change the sieves as the need arises.

For young chicks, use a 2mm sieve

Crushing should be done collectively and not separately. Grind all the ingredients together and not separately. This enhances good mixing right from the point of crushing.

For Adults chicken use a 5-6mm sieve

A crusher with changeable sieves (electrical)

Example of sieve

A petrol-powered crusher is able to crush all types of feed ingredients to different particle sizes as desired. This type of crusher is good for farmers in areas without electricity.

42

A crusher connected by conveyor to the mixer.

CHARACTERISTICS OF A GOOD CRUSHER

It is very efficient - crushing 1-2 tons
(s) per hour
It's economical
It doesn't waste feed ingredient
It comes with changeable sieves
Its components should be easy to lose
and tight as required.

Step 8

MIXING AND BAGGING

Mixing is a method of uniformly distributing different ingredients in the formula in the feed.

Thoroughly mix all ingredients until homogeneous (when it is difficult to identify individual ingredients)

It is very necessary to pre-mix all additives before adding them to the bulk ingredients. If you pour additives directly into the mixer, they will settle at the bottom or base of the mixer.

This is accomplished by taking a specific amount (approximately 5kg) of bulk ingredients and mixing them separately with the additives (lysine, methionine, salt, enzyme...), and then spread the mixture over the entire

ingredients. You can mix manually or with an electric mixer.

If your feed is not well mixed, some of your chicken may receive more of one ingredient and less of another, which means your chicken will develop at different rates.

The next thing after mixing is to discharge the feed from the mixer.

Your feed can be mixed manually through the following stages

✓ pour out the crushed feed on a well-cemented floor

✓ Measure out all your additives in a bowl

✓ Add about 2-3kg of the feed to the additives and thoroughly mix them. This is called premixing.

✓ Spread the premixed on the entire feed uniformly.

✓ Use shovel to mix everything until homogeneous mixture is achieved

✓ Bag your feed

This is an electrical operated mixer